Popular Cat Library

Exotic Shorthair Cat

Karen Commings

Published in association with T.F.H. Publications, Inc.,
the world's largest and most respected publisher of pet literature

Chelsea House Publishers
Philadelphia

CONTENTS

Popular Cat Library

Abyssinian Cat
American Shorthair Cat
Bengal Cat
Birman Cat
Burmese Cat
Exotic Shorthair Cat
Himalayan Cat
Maine Coon Cat
Persian Cat
Ragdoll Cat
Scottish Fold Cat
Siamese Cat

Publisher's Note: All of the photographs in this book have been coated with FOTO-GLAZE® finish, a special lamination that imparts a new dimension of colorful gloss to the photographs.

Reinforced Library Binding & Super-Highest Quality Boards

This edition © TFH Publications, Inc., 1 TFH Plaza, Neptune City, NJ 07753. This special library bound edition is made expressly for Chelsea House Publishers, a division of Main Line Book Company.

Library of Congress Cataloging-in-Publication Data

Commings, Karen.
Guide to owning an exotic shorthair / by Karen Commings.
p.   cm. — (Popular cat library)
Summary: A guide to the history, feeding, grooming, exhibition, temperament, health, and breeding of Exotic Shorthair cats.
ISBN 0-7910-5462-4 (hc.)
1. Exotic shorthair cat Juvenile literature.   [1. Exotic shorthair cat. 2. Cats.
3. Pets.]   I. Title. II. Series.
SF449.E93C86 1999
636.8'2—dc21   99-36714
                                            CIP

The Guide to Owning an
Exotic
Shorthair Cat

Karen Commings

CONTENTS

Photography: Gil Arellanes, Larry Bellotti, Karen Commings, Isabelle Francais, Pam Hill, Rick Parker, Grace Thomas, Flora Thurston

Title Page: Ch. Grand Premier Echo Hill Roxanne, owned by Pam Hill

RE-412

© T.F.H. Publications, Inc.

Distributed in the UNITED STATES to the Pet Trade by T.F.H. Publications, Inc., 1 TFH Plaza, Neptune City, NJ 07753; on the Internet at www.tfh.com; in CANADA by Rolf C. Hagen Inc., 3225 Sartelon St., Montreal, Quebec H4R 1E8; Pet Trade by H & L Pet Supplies Inc., 27 Kingston Crescent, Kitchener, Ontario N2B 2T6; in ENGLAND by T.F.H. Publications, PO Box 74, Havant PO9 5TT; in AUSTRALIA AND THE SOUTH PACIFIC by T.F.H. (Australia), Pty. Ltd., Box 149, Brookvale 2100 N.S.W., Australia; in NEW ZEALAND by Brooklands Aquarium Ltd., 5 McGiven Drive, New Plymouth, RD1 New Zealand; in SOUTH AFRICA by Rolf C. Hagen S.A. (PTY.) LTD., P.O. Box 201199, Durban North 4016, South Africa; in JAPAN by T.F.H. Publications, Japan—Jiro Tsuda, 10-12-3 Ohjidai, Sakura, Chiba 285, Japan. Published by T.F.H. Publications, Inc. MANUFACTURED IN THE UNITED STATES OF AMERICA BY T.F.H. PUBLICATIONS, INC.

HISTORY OF THE EXOTIC SHORTHAIR

Not all cats come straight from Mother Nature. The exquisite Exotic Shorthair, sweet-faced and serene feline that she is, can thank human intervention for her development and existence. In the 1960s, breeders of what were then called Domestic Shorthairs wanted to improve the breed. To accomplish their goals, they began outcrossing the Domestic Shorthair with silver Persians to obtain the same lovely, shaded silver coat for their own cats. The resulting felines, with their flatter faces, larger and rounder eyes, and their plusher and fuller coats in colors unheard of in the Domestic Shorthair line, were more pleasing to the eye of the beholder, whether it was the breeder or the show judge. Even though they did not conform to the Domestic Shorthair standard, the new cats on the block were more successful in competition with other Domestic Shorthairs that did not have Persian in their bloodlines.

THE EARLY DAYS

Because of the unique appearance of the yet unnamed Exotic Shorthair, a controversy

In the 1960s, breeders outcrossed the Domestic Shorthair with silver Persians to create a new breed, called the Exotic Shorthair.

developed in the Cat Fanciers' Association (CFA) among both American Shorthair breeders and breeders of Persians. While the new look caught the judges' attention, they turned a blind eye to the new Persian colors and thick, luxurious coats making their way into the Domestic program. Taking notice of the new, hybridized cats being shown in the Domestic Shorthair class, they wrote a letter requesting the CFA to establish a new breed category to accommodate them. That same year, the Domestic Shorthair became the American Shorthair in the CFA. By

The Exotic Shorthair has a flatter face, larger and rounder eyes, and a plusher, fuller coat than the Domestic Shorthair. Supreme Ch. Sweetpeacats Carousel, owned by Grace Thomas.

Shorthair line, as well as to the fuller, more rounded appearance of this new, hybridized cat making its way into the cat fancy. Once introduced into the Domestic Shorthair lines, the fluffier coats couldn't be gotten rid of. In 1966, Richard H. Gebhardt, international all-breed judge and member of the CFA board of directors, and Jane Martinke, a CFA all-breed judge, were co-chairs of the CFA's breed establishing a new breed, the now outcrossed American Shorthairs would be legalized and have a place within the fancy. The proposed name of the breed was Sterling, derived from the silver coat, and the original intent was to have cats transfer from the American Shorthair class to the new breed category if they had been outcrossed with Persians. The new breed, ultimately called Exotic

Shorthair, was accepted first among the cat registries by the CFA and achieved championship status on May 1, 1967.

ALONG THE WAY

Although the original intent of crossing an American Shorthair with a Persian was to improve the American Shorthair type, once breeders created the teddy bear look of the Exotic Shorthair, it became obvious that what people wanted was really a short-haired Persian with the same appealing face, but a short coat that was

Not only is the Exotic's teddy bear look very appealing, but her shorter coat is easy to care for and groom.

easier to care for and groom. To get that plush coat, early Exotic Shorthair breeders outcrossed to other breeds besides the American Shorthair, introducing Burmese and Russian Blues into their Exotic Shorthair pedigrees. If a breeder wanted to achieve an Shorthair back to the Persian to get closer to the Persian standard and type. The practice of outcrossing with any registered shorthair in the CFA continued until 1975, at which time the CFA closed the registry to permit only American Shorthair and

The Exotic Shorthair, increasingly popular among breeders and pet owners, first achieved championship status in 1967. Ch. Echo Hill Saturn, a shaded silver male, owned by Pam Hill.

Exotic Shorthair with a pointed coat pattern, he or she crossed with a Himalayan. Although more than one breed played a part in giving the Exotic Shorthair her short coat, once the short coat was introduced into a bloodline, the breeder took the Exotic Persian outcrosses. In 1987, the CFA changed the rules again, permitting only outcrosses to Persians.

The wheels of change sometimes move slowly, and within the cat fancy, acceptance of this new breed was no exception. Persian breeders resisted when early breeders of Exotic Shorthairs wanted to obtain stud Persians to enter into their breeding programs. One of the early Exotic Shorthair national winners, Docia-Dao's Trilby, a black smoke kitten bred and owned by Barbara and Don Yoder, did more to change the opinions of Persian breeders than all of the Exotic Shorthair breeders could have done at the time. The Yoders bred Persians as well as Exotics, and the success of their kitten, which went on to win national championships as an adult, made Persian breeders stop and take a second look at this new line of short-coated cats. As the Exotic Shorthair became more popular, Persian breeders became more willing to allow their cats to be used in the Exotic Shorthair pedigree.

THE LOOK

The early Exotic Shorthairs, like their Persian counterparts of the time, looked different than they do today. Instead of a nose break (the indentation in the nose running between the eyes), Exotic Shorthairs had a nose. The ears varied and were often more upright instead of to the side and tilting forward, due to the introduction of different short-haired cats into the Exotic Shorthair pedigree. Their legs were longer and their bodies and tails more like the American Shorthair than the Persian.

From the start, the standard of the Exotic Shorthair was intended to be the same as the Persian, and it evolved along with the Persian standard in the CFA. As the new breed evolved and came closer in appearance to its Persian ancestor, the standard was redefined in 1990 to make it the same as the Persian, except for the short coat. It was at that time that the CFA changed the name of the Exotic Shorthair to simply the "Exotic."

Breeding Exotic Shorthairs can be challenging, because the results of a mating in terms of coat length can be so unpredictable. Because the long-hair gene is recessive, the result of an Exotic Shorthair and Persian mating will produce some living, breathing oxymorons—long-haired Exotic Shorthairs. Long-haired kittens may be used in a breeding program, but must mate with another short-haired Exotic to produce short-haired kittens. As difficult to read as a multideck card game, the homozygous Exotic that produces only short-haired kittens even when bred to a long-haired cat is an ideal that Exotic breeders long for but have difficulty attaining. Some breed associations, such as The International Cat Association (TICA), allow long-haired Exotic Shorthairs to be shown in competition. For CFA members, the long-haired Exotic has no place to compete.

Since its appearance on the scene in the 1960s, the Exotic Shorthair has steadily grown in popularity among breeders and the pet-owning public.

CHARACTER AND PERSONALITY

Once you've gazed into those saucer-shaped eyes and felt the plush coat that is characteristic of the Exotic Shorthair, it's easy to understand the concept of love at first sight. The Exotic Shorthair has one of the sweetest faces and softest coats among the many breeds of cat. You'll be happy to learn that her personality is just as captivating and her character just as giving to her human companions.

body that is thicker and more massive than the Persian's. They have been described as a "Persian in a wet T-shirt" and their thick, soft coats have the feel of a plush bathroom rug.

A HARDY BREED

Breeders of Exotic Shorthairs believe the cats to be healthy, robust, and hardier than a lot of breeds due to their expanded gene pool, which has included the

The Exotic is intelligent, sweet-natured, pensive, and an ideal apartment cat. Similar to a Persian in temperament, she can be relaxed and aloof one minute, and a fun-loving extrovert the next. Ch. Sunny Sky's Steele, a blue Exotic male, owned by Gil Arellanes, Arealand Cattery.

With Exotic Shorthairs, *round* seems to be the operative word. They have large, round eyes that are set far apart. Their heads and faces, too, are round, complementing a round, cobby

American Shorthair, Russian Blue, and Burmese, in addition to Persian bloodlines. Breeders familiar with the Persian side of the family say that it's the addition of the short-hair gene

Exotic kittens are inquisitive, loving, and mischievous—and like being the center of attention. Ch. Sweetpeacats Kewpie and her babies, owned by Grace Thomas.

that makes the difference in temperament and soundness. Persian kittens are born smaller and need closer attention, while the Exotic Shorthair seems to be born walking. The Exotics' eyes open faster, they walk quicker, play sooner, and wean earlier than their Persian cousins. In appearance, they resemble fat, chunky caterpillars at birth and thrive from that moment on.

EXOTIC SHORTHAIR KITTENS

Exotic kittens are playful, inquisitive, alert, loving, and mischievous—other traits they inherited from their American Shorthair ancestry. Expect them to stalk everything that moves,

from crickets to houseflies. Exotic Shorthair kittens enjoy jumping in the air after a feather tease, chasing each other, your children, or the family dog, and playing floor hockey with whatever rolls. Because Exotic Shorthair kittens are more inquisitive, they get themselves into things and, consequently, into more trouble. A Persian kitten may never climb your curtains, but that may not be true of an Exotic Shorthair.

They will fetch and can be taught tricks, such as lying down to be slid across the linoleum floor and coming back to slide again and again. After they've zoomed around your house for 20 minutes or so, they drop where they are for a quick catnap. As an Exotic Shorthair's human caregiver, you're expected to walk around or step over them, because they aren't going to move.

So captivating and appealing are Exotic Shorthair kittens that you may just find them stealing the show whenever you have visitors. They like company and are social, so it's not unusual for them to want to be the center of attention, making themselves at home on your guests' laps as well as your own.

They are usually very playful, even into old age. They readily sleep on your pillow at night, knead their toes on your head or other exposed body parts, and stalk your toes under the covers, sometimes waking you from sleep for a game of pounce. Your Exotic Shorthair is likely to watch television with you, and just try to read a book without your Exotic Shorthair trying to get between you and your reading material.

Like most domestic animals, an Exotic Shorthair is going to be

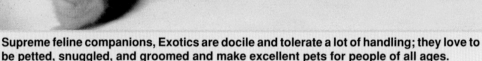

Supreme feline companions, Exotics are docile and tolerate a lot of handling; they love to be petted, snuggled, and groomed and make excellent pets for people of all ages.

EXOTIC SHORTHAIR ADULTS

The adult Exotic Shorthair is very similar to the kitten and most likely will retain her kittenish temperament even after experiencing parenthood. They run and romp with their kittens, training them at the same time.

very happy with a human of any age, as long as she is treated with the proper care and attention. These cats make excellent pets for families with children or for senior citizens. Although the Exotic Shorthair is more boisterous than her Persian cousin, breeders say that she makes a wonderful pet for anyone who likes living with a jovial animal, as opposed to one that is frenetic—a quiet sense of humor as opposed to high hilarity.

If you appreciate the feel of a very substantial but not overly large cat without a coat that demands much grooming or that emits clouds of hair, you will find the Exotic Shorthair very appealing. Exotic Shorthairs are very loyal and love to be groomed, petted, hugged, and snuggled. They are docile and tolerate a lot of handling. So complacent are they that you may find your children dressing them up in their doll clothes and carrying them around or letting them play with their action figures. They are pretty tough and rugged and aren't defensive or aggressive, but as with all pets, children should be taught to respect them and handle them gently.

Exotic Shorthairs are peaceful and, for the most part quiet, although you may find your Exotic Shorthair asking you outright for what she wants. When these cats talk, you may hear a lot of chirping and meowing. Most of them have the quiet, high-pitched voice of a Persian, which is quite at odds with their more substantial body types. They want your attention and will be very vocal if they don't get it.

Exotic Shorthairs really enjoy human company and would much rather be with humans than other cats. When caged, they do not give up voicing their discomfort at being locked away from you. Expect your Exotic Shorthair to be sensitive to you and your needs, comforting you if you feel upset by sitting with or on you. They are affectionate and like to snuggle—in bed or on the couch. You may find your cat wrapping her paws around your neck for a hug or burying her face in your neck to nestle, but don't be disconcerted if she doesn't always want to sit on your lap, preferring instead to chase a bug around the room. Of course be prepared to hear lots of that wonderful feline purring when you and your Exotic Shorthair share some quiet moments together.

Although often peaceful and quiet, your Exotic will be very vocal when she wants your attention and isn't getting it. Preferring human company, this hardy breed is usually active and playful, even into old age.

THE EXOTIC STANDARD AND COLORS

A truly excellent example of the Exotic Shorthair is something to behold. Her appearance is just like her Persian cousin, but without the long coat. The Exotic been established by the association in which they are registered. Simply stated, breed standards are ideals of appearance against which each

An ideal Exotic Shorthair is a sight to behold. Her appearance is similar to her cousin, the Persian, but without the long coat.

Shorthair has a massive and cobby, densely boned body, with huge eyes and an intense gaze. The coat on the Exotic resembles a plush teddy bear, and her undercoat is dense enough to make the guard hairs stand away from her body.

THE STANDARD

Anyone who has watched an Olympic gymnastics meet or skating competition knows that competitors have a standard of quality against which their performances are judged. Likewise, cats entering show competitions are evaluated against a breed standard that has cat is judged. The winning cat in each category should most closely match the standard for her breed.

If you have a pet-quality Exotic, she will provide you with the same love and companionship as a show-quality one, but if you are planning to compete in cat shows, it is best to familiarize yourself with the standards for the breed and learn to recognize an outstanding specimen.

Each cat registry applies a certain number of points to each of the various features based on their relative importance. Judges, however, don't mentally add up the points for each cat in the show ring as they are judging.

Rather, they look for features that don't conform to breed standards and might disqualify them.

EXOTIC BREED STANDARD

The Exotic Shorthair standards may vary slightly from registry to registry. Unlike the dog fancy, which is governed exclusively by the American Kennel Club, the cat

size, bone, and length of tail) ... 20
COAT 10
BALANCE 5
REFINEMENT 5
COLOR 20
EYE COLOR 10
For cats in the tabby division, the 20 points for color are to be divided ten for markings and ten for color. For cats in the bicolor

A cobby, heavily-boned, well-balanced cat, the Exotic has a sweet expression and soft, round lines.

fancy has several US and Canadian registries that track the lineage, or pedigree, of the members' cats. The largest registry in the world is the Cat Fanciers' Association, and it is the CFA standard that is reproduced here with permission. Because the Exotic Shorthair is called simply, "Exotic" by the CFA, the term Exotic is used throughout this chapter.

POINT SCORE

HEAD (including size and shape of eyes; ear shape and set) 30
BODY TYPE (including shape,

division, the 20 points for color are to be divided ten for "with white" pattern and ten for color.

GENERAL: The ideal Exotic should present an impression of a heavily boned, well-balanced cat with a sweet expression and soft, round lines. The large, round eyes set wide apart in a large round head contribute to the overall look and expression. The thick, plush coat softens the lines of the cat and accentuates the roundness in appearance.

HEAD: Round and massive,

Longer than the typical Shorthair's, an Exotic's coat grows dense and plush and has a soft, silky texture. Standing out from the body and medium in length, the thick fur accentuates the cat's roundness in appearance.

with great breadth of skull. Round face with round underlying bone structure. Well set on a short, thick neck.

NOSE: Short, snub, and broad, with "break" centered between the eyes.

CHEEKS: Full.

JAWS: Broad and powerful.

CHIN: Full, well-developed, and firmly rounded, reflecting a proper bite.

EARS: Small, round tipped, tilted forward, and not unduly open at the base. Set far apart, and low on the head, fitting into (without distorting) the rounded contour of the head.

EYES: Brilliant in color, large, round, and full. Set level and far apart, giving a sweet expression to the face.

The Exotic Shorthair can be seen in almost every color known to cats. The CFA recognizes 70 colors, combinations, and coat patterns, which are all part of the Exotic standard.

This black Exotic has large, round, brilliant copper eyes, which are a striking feature of the breed.

BODY: Of cobby type, low on the legs, broad and deep through the chest, equally massive across the shoulders and rump, with a well-rounded midsection and level back. Good muscle tone, with no evidence of obesity. Large or medium in size. Quality the determining consideration rather than size.

LEGS: Short, thick, and strong. Forelegs straight. Hind legs straight when viewed from behind.

PAWS: Large, round, and firm. Toes carried close, five in front and four behind.

TAIL: Short, but in proportion to body length. Carried without a curve and at an angle lower than the back.

COAT: Dense, plush, soft, and full of life. Standing out from the body due to a rich, thick undercoat. Medium in length. Acceptable length depends on proper undercoat. Cats with a ruff or tail-feathers (long hair on the tail) shall be transferred to the Any Other Variety class.

DISQUALIFY: Locket or button. Kinked or abnormal tail. Incorrect number of toes. Any apparent weakness in the hindquarters. Any apparent deformity of the spine. Deformity of the skull resulting in an asymmetrical face and/or head. Crossed eyes. For pointed cats, disqualify for white toes, eye color other than blue.

EXOTIC COLORS

Acceptable colors are also part of the Exotic standard. The CFA recognizes approximately 70 Exotic colors, color combinations and coat patterns. Breeders often try to develop new colors, so the list may grow if a new color is approved by the registry. Some colors, like white and black, bear names that even a newcomer to the cat fancy will understand. Others, such as chinchilla silver and chinchilla golden, chocolate van calico, blue-cream smoke, lilac patched tabby, and shaded cream are as exotic as the breed itself.

In the cat fancy, the names used to describe some colors are not what the average person is accustomed to calling them. For example, what most cat owners commonly refer to as a gray cat is called *blue* in the cat fancy. Cats that look orange are called *red*. If a cat's eyes appear to be orange, they are called *copper*. The word lilac defines a cat with a lavender or pinkish coat, while chocolate is used to describe a coat that is brown. If that seems confusing, add to it the degrees or types of coloring (van, shell, shaded and smoke) the coat patterns (tabbies, calicos and tortoiseshells) and it becomes obvious that you will find Exotics in a virtual crazy quilt of varieties

The Exotic is judged against the Persian standard for body type. Red tabby Exotic, owned by Rick Parker.

that only those heavily involved in breeding, showing, and judging could ever remember without the help of a printed list.

The color standards are quite specific and define not only which colors are acceptable but also where on the cat's body they should appear. Because the color standards are very detailed, it is impossible to provide a comprehensive list of them here, but a sampling will give the Exotic owner a glimpse into the world of the cat fancy as the CFA defines it.

SOLID COLORS

WHITE: Pure glistening white. **Nose leather and paw pads:** pink. **Eye color:** deep blue or brilliant copper.

BLUE: Blue, lighter shade preferred, one level tone from nose to tip of tail. Sound to the roots. **Nose leather and paw pads:** blue. **Eye color:** brilliant copper.

BLACK: Dense coal black, sound from roots to tip of fur. Free from any tinge of rust on tips or smoke undercoat. **Nose leather:** black. **Paw pads:** black or brown. **Eye color:** brilliant copper.

CHOCOLATE: Rich, warm chocolate-brown, sound from roots to tip of fur. **Nose leather:** brown. **Paw pads:** cinnamon-pink. **Eye color:** brilliant copper.

CREAM: One level shade of buff cream, without markings. Sound to the roots. Lighter shades preferred. **Nose leather and paw pads:** pink. **Eye color:** brilliant copper.

PEKE-FACE RED: The peke-face cat should conform in color and general type to the standard set forth for the red cat; however, allowance should be made for the slightly higher placement of the ears to conform with the underlying bone structure of the head, which differs greatly from that of the standard Exotic. The nose

Bicolor Exotics have coats that are white combined with another color.

LILAC: Rich, warm lavender with a pinkish tone, sound and even throughout. **Nose leather and paw pads:** lavender-pink. **Eye color:** brilliant copper.

RED: Deep, rich, clear, brilliant red; without shading, markings, or ticking. Lips and chin the same color as coat. **Nose leather and paw pads:** brick red. **Eye color:** brilliant copper.

should be short, depressed, and indented between the eyes. The muzzle should be wrinkled. Eyes should be large, round, and set wide apart. The horizontal break, which is located between the usual nose break and the top dome of the head, runs straight across the front of the head, creating half-moon boning above the eyes and an additional horizontal indentation located in

Color standards are quite specific, defining which colors are acceptable and where they should appear on the cat's body. Tortoiseshell Exotic kitten.

the center of the forehead bone structure. This bone structure results in a very round head with a strong chin. Eyes brilliant copper.

BICOLORS

Bicolors are cats with coats that are white combined with another color. Acceptable color combinations are black and white, blue and white, red and white, cream and white, chocolate and white, and lilac and white. As a preferred minimum, the cat should have white feet, legs, undersides, chest, and muzzle. Less white than this minimum should be penalized proportionately. Inverted "V" blaze on face is desirable. Eyes should be brilliant copper, blue, or odd-eyed. Odd-eyed bicolors are to have one blue and one copper eye with equal color depth.

PARTICOLOR COLORS

Particolors are cats with coats that are white combined with coat patterns or combinations of colors (blue-cream, calico, dilute calico, tabby and white, tortoiseshell, van bicolor, van calico, or van dilute calico).

POINTED COLORS

Pointed cats usually have a cream, bluish, or fawn-colored body, with point color primarily confined to the face, ears, legs, and tail. Pointed cats must have a body color that corresponds to the darker color of the points. Acceptable Exotic pointed colors are blue lynx point, blue point, blue-cream point, chocolate point, lilac point, lilac-cream point, seal lynx point, seal point, and tortie point.

SHADED COLORS

Cats with a shaded coat have an undercoat that is white with a mantle of tipping that shades down her sides. Acceptable Exotic shaded colors are chinchilla golden and chinchilla silver, shaded cameo, shaded golden, shaded silver, and shaded tortoiseshell.

SMOKE COLORS

Smoke defines cats with a white undercoat that is tipped in the cat's basic color so that when they are in repose they appear to be that color. When they are in motion, the white undercoat becomes apparent. Acceptable Exotic smoke colors are black smoke, blue smoke, blue-cream smoke, cameo smoke, and tortoiseshell smoke.

SHELL COLORS

Shell defines a cat with a white undercoat, with the coat on her back, flanks, head, and tail lightly tipped with her basic color. Face and legs may be lightly shaded with tipping. Frill, ear tufts, stomach, and chest are white.

van colors are van calico, van dilute calico, chocolate van calico, lilac van calico, bicolor van, van smoke and white, and van tabby and white.

TABBY COLORS

As with the van, tabby describes a coat pattern. Tabby cats come in both the mackerel tabby pattern and the classic, or blotched, tabby pattern. The CFA recognizes both patterns in the Exotic.

The mackerel tabby cat has dense, clearly defined markings and all narrow pencillings. Legs are evenly barred with narrow bracelets coming up to meet the body markings. The tail is barred. Necklaces on the neck

Tabby describes a coat pattern; this brown mackerel tabby has dense, clearly defined markings and narrow pencillings.

VAN COLORS

Van describes a color pattern in which the cat has color confined to her head, tail, and legs as in the Turkish Van breed, with one or two allowable spots of color on her body. Acceptable

and chest are distinct, like so many chains. Head is barred with an "M" on the forehead. Unbroken lines run back from the eyes. Lines run down the head to meet the shoulders. Spine lines run together to form a narrow saddle.

A classic red tabby will have frown marks on her forehead that form an intricate letter "M" and a large solid blotch on each side of her body encircled by one or more unbroken rings.

The classic tabby pattern has dense, clearly defined, and broad markings that are swirled rather than striped. The legs are evenly barred with bracelets coming up to meet the body markings. Tail is evenly ringed. Several unbroken necklaces on neck and upper chest, the more the better. Frown marks on forehead form an intricate letter "M." Unbroken line runs back from outer corner of the eye. Swirls on cheeks. Vertical lines over back of head extend to shoulder markings, which are in the shape of a butterfly, with both upper and lower wings distinctly outlined and marked with dots inside outline. Back markings consist of a vertical line down the spine from butterfly to tail with a vertical stripe paralleling it on each side, the three stripes well separated by stripes of the ground color. Large solid blotch on each side to be encircled by one or more unbroken rings. Side markings should be the same on both sides. Double vertical rows of buttons on chest and stomach.

Acceptable Exotic tabby colors are silver, silver patched, blue silver, blue silver patched, red, peke-face red, brown, brown patched, blue, blue patched, cream, cameo, cream cameo, chocolate, chocolate patched, lilac, and lilac patched.

CALICOS AND TORTOISESHELLS

A calico cat is white with unbrindled patches of black and red on her body. A dilute calico is a white cat with unbrindled patches of blue and cream. White is predominant on the underparts. Tortoiseshells have unbrindled patches of red and cream combined with some other color such as black or chestnut. Because the gene that carries the calico pattern is a sex-linked gene, calicos and torties are almost always female. The occasional male produced will be sterile.

EYE COLOR

Exotics can have a variety of eye colors that are acceptable in the show ring. The breed standard specifies for each coat color and pattern the appropriate eye colors.

Ch. Sweetpeacats Kimella and Sweetpeacats Jade, award-winning calicos owned by Grace Thomas.

SELECTING AN EXOTIC SHORTHAIR

Now that you've decided that the exquisite Exotic Shorthair is the cat for you, your next step is to make some decisions about what kind of Exotic Shorthair you want. A little bit of planning will go a long way in helping find a cat suitable for you and keep you from making any costly mistakes that you may later regret.

KITTEN AND CAT

The first decision you should make is what age your cat will be.

People love kittens. They are playful, inquisitive, and fun to watch. Kittens are thought to come with no bad habits and no retraining requirements. Even so, the drawback to adopting a kitten is that because your home is her playground, she will require more constant attention and energy than an older, more mature adult cat.

The adult cat, on the other hand, is one that has a developed appearance and personality. When you purchase an adult cat, what you see is what you get. No guesswork is involved in determining how the cat will turn out. If you are interested in exhibiting, the quality and

Before choosing a pet, remember that a kitten will require constant attention and more energy than an older, mature adult.

Kitten or adult cat? A bit of research and planning will help you select a cat of an age suitable for your lifestyle.

conformation to breed standards of an adult cat will be apparent. For the potential exhibitor, purchasing an adult that has competed in the ring a few times will help simplify the process of finding a show cat.

If simply finding a healthy companion animal is your primary concern, an adult will offer the same love and affection as a kitten. Breeders often sell as pets the adult cats that are no

MALE OR FEMALE

Generalizing about differences in the feline sexes is as untenable as generalizing about the human ones. Just when you think you have a rule of thumb, someone comes along and points to an exception. Given an environment filled with love and affection, both male and female cats will make great pets.

If you are planning on becoming a breeder, finding a top-quality

If you are planning to become a breeder, finding a top-quality female should be your priority. Ch. Sweetpeacats Kewpie and her four kittens sired by Dbl. Ch. Softpaws Spuds McKay of Sweetpeacats, owned by Grace Thomas.

longer part of the show circuit or their breeding program. The price may occasionally be less than for a kitten. The disadvantages to purchasing an adult are that you will not be able to shape her character and personality or watch your cat grow up. Although the cattery environment will play an important part in her ability to adjust to her new home, an adult cat may take longer than a kitten.

female should be your primary concern. Stud service may be provided by a male under contract from another cattery. Intact male cats engage in territorial spray marking, resulting in a characteristic cat odor that is offensive and difficult to eliminate. Keeping an unneutered male in your home can cause problems you may not want to deal with, unless you are committed to

It's easier to tell if a cat is show quality if she's older and has a proven history in the show ring.

becoming a breeder or can find a separate location in your home in which to maintain the cat.

The sex you choose will ultimately be a matter of personal preference. Breeders say male cats tend to be affectionate lap cats that can be depended on, once a bond of trust is established, to seek out their owners consistently for petting sessions or attention. While just as affectionate, a female might want your attention one minute and be rather aloof the next. Your cat, no doubt, will be the exception to the rule.

PET OR SHOW

The vast majority of kittens available for purchase, even from reputable breeders, are what is commonly referred to as pet-quality—those kittens that do not conform to the breed standard in some way. The lack of conformation simply may be that a cat's color or coat pattern is not one that is accepted by the association in which she is registered. Don't be misled into thinking that a pet-quality kitten is in some way substandard or that, if you purchase one, her life will be full of health-related problems. A cat's lack of conformation will only be a problem if you intend to exhibit your cat, in which case, the more closely she conforms to the standard, the better chance you have of successfully competing.

Most breeders keep their kittens until they are 12 to 16 weeks of age. During that time, they are able to assess the kittens and determine which ones may make the best show cats. Breeders typically keep the best quality kittens in a litter for part of their own breeding programs, so purchasing a show-quality cat is more difficult than purchasing a pet-quality one. It's easier to tell if a cat is show quality if she is older and has a proven history in the show ring. If showing or breeding is your intention, ask the breeder to see the kitten's pedigree. Find out how many champions the sire and dam have produced and what titles other members of her family have produced. Ask to see cats with a proven track record.

will help ensure that you find a healthy cat to be your companion for a long time. If showing or breeding Exotic Shorthairs is in your future, it is imperative that you find a reputable breeder from whom to buy a cat that is free of contagious diseases and conforms to the standard of the breed.

Pet shops care little about where their animals come from

Finding a reputable breeder from which to purchase your Exotic Shorthair will ensure that you have a healthy, longtime companion.

WHERE TO BUY

Although you will be able to find kittens from an array of sources—pet shops, newspaper ads, breeders, and maybe even the person in the cubicle next to you at the office, it can't be stressed too much that finding a reputable breeder from which to purchase your Exotic Shorthair

and where they go. Because responsible breeders want to make sure their kittens are placed in good homes with people who can adequately care for them, they screen prospective buyers. Pet shops care only that the buyer has the money to pay for the kitten. Because responsible breeders often belong to clubs with codes of ethics prohibiting members from selling kittens to pet shops, these shops are forced to rely on kitten and puppy mills—commercial kennels that churn out kittens and puppies simply to make a profit. Females live in cages and are kept pregnant whenever they are in heat, which can be three to four times a year. Because profit is the motive, little money is spent on veterinary care and adequate nutrition for the needs of the pregnant female or her offspring. You as the buyer will never see where the cat came from and under what kind of conditions she was born and raised.

Pet shops also rely on the backyard breeder as suppliers—the person who has a purebred female cat and, for whatever reason, wants her to have a litter of kittens. Like the mills, backyard breeders care little about the health and well-being of the offspring and where they will be placed, much less whether the kittens conform to a breed standard.

To find reputable breeders, look

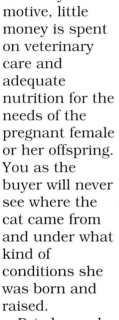

Responsible breeders make sure their kittens are placed in good homes.

in the directories of the major cat magazines. Most of the national registries offer breeder referral lines that will point you to breeders in your geographic area. The major registries also have a presence on the World Wide Web and list breeders by breed and by state. Ask your veterinarian if he or she is familiar with any in your area. Look in the pets columns of your local newspapers. Contact a local cat club and attend a show, not only to find breeders, but to see the kinds of cats they produce.

Once you have located some breeders, visit their catteries. Some registries, such as the CFA, have cattery inspection programs, which means that the catteries have been inspected by veterinarians and adhere to specific standards. The program is voluntary, and breeders must pay an inspection fee to the veterinarian and a certification fee to the CFA. The certification is good for one year from the time of inspection.

You will learn a lot about the quality of the cats produced in a

Two litters of Exotic kittens at one month of age. Ample socialization with humans helps a kitten adjust to life as a companion animal and ensures that she'll seek out contact as an adult.

cattery just by visiting it and asking questions of the breeder. Do the cats appear healthy? Do they appear to conform to the breed standard? Are the cats and kittens socialized with humans or do they stay in cages? The first two to three weeks of a cat's life are the most impressionable, and early socialization plays an important role in developing the personality of a cat. It is during this time that the most important part of the socialization process takes place. Kittens left alone to amuse themselves will continue to do so as they become adults, whereas the kitten that has enjoyed human contact as an important part of her life will continue to seek out that contact as an adult. If the breeder is a good one, he or she will have

provided the kittens with ample human contact to help them adjust to life as companion animals. What are the conditions under which the queen and her offspring are kept? Are pregnant females and kittens given food that meets the special nutritional requirements of their condition and age?

Expect the breeder to ask questions of you, too. Good breeders invest a lot of time, effort, and money into their cats and kittens and will want to know if you can continue to provide them with excellent care. You will also be required to sign a contract at the time of purchase that will require you to have the cat you purchase spayed or neutered, unless a legitimate breeding program is in your plans.

If the nearest cattery is too far away to visit, ask the breeder to send you photos of the kittens available. Most breeders will ship a kitten to you if you cannot come to get it. Regardless of the cattery's location, ask the breeder to give you references. People who have purchased kittens or cats from the breeder will be able to offer you insight into the relative quality of the cats they bought.

routinely tested for contagious diseases. Reputable breeders offer a guarantee that the kitten will remain healthy for a specified time period after purchase; if she does not, she may be replaced or your money refunded.

Healthy kittens and cats will be alert. Take along a toy and watch to see if the kitten follows it attentively. A healthy kitten's eyes will be bright, shiny, and clear

You can learn a lot about the quality of cats produced in a cattery by visiting it and asking the breeder questions. Ch. Chinchelita Sasha of Sweetpeacats and her seven babies, owned by Grace Thomas.

A HEALTHY CAT

If the breeder is a good one, you can be sure of obtaining a healthy cat. By the time a kitten is offered for sale, she has been weaned, is eating solid food, has received the first set of vaccinations, and has visited a veterinarian at least once. Cattery animals are

with no watery discharge. Her ears will be clean. Her coat will have no bald patches or evidence of flea dirt, and the area around her tail will be clean. The shorter nose of the Exotic Shorthair may tend to close the nose up slightly, so you are advised to find a kitten with larger nostrils.

GENERAL CARE AND GROOMING

Before bringing home your Exotic Shorthair, you will need to purchase some basic necessities. First and foremost is a litter box. Litter boxes come in all shapes and sizes. Even if your Exotic Shorthair is a kitten or small adult, a larger litter box will provide her with ample room to turn around and dig—a feline favorite pastime—and prevent you from having to invest in a larger box as your cat grows. If your home or apartment is small, you might want to buy a covered box or hide it completely by purchasing one of the newer litter boxes concealed in a piece of furniture. If your local pet store does not carry the kind of box you want, check in the classified sections of the major cat magazines at the newsstand.

You'll find just as many types of cat box filler as you will litter boxes. Clay or clumping litter, litter made from newspaper pellets, corn cobs, or wood chips—the variety is endless. Some filler requires disposal with the rest of your garbage, while other types can be flushed down the toilet. Cats seem to develop preferences for certain types of litter. Perhaps one is less dusty or softer on their feet. When you purchase your Exotic Shorthair, find out from the breeder the kind of litter to which she is accustomed, then make any

Although cats are more independent than many other pets, they still require the proper care and attention necessary to stay healthy and fit.

changes gradually to prevent litter box aversion problems.

Cats are naturally drawn to anything in which they can dig and bury their wastes, so your Exotic Shorthair kitten will already know how to use the box when you purchase it. To help your new kitten or cat learn where the box is, show her the box immediately when you bring her home. Keeping the litter box clean is the best way to ensure that the pads of their feet. Some cat owners have their cats declawed, a procedure whereby the toenails, usually on the front feet, are surgically removed. You may be under contract with the breeder from whom you purchased your Exotic Shorthair not to have her declawed. If you intend to show your cat, her claws must be intact. Cats are drawn as naturally to scratching posts as they are to their litter boxes, so

Before bringing one of these cute kittens home, you will need to provide some basic necessities: a litter box, food and water bowls, and perhaps a soft, foam bed.

your cat continues to use it, so purchase a slotted litter scoop and remove wastes daily.

In addition to digging, scratching is another favorite feline occupation. Scratching enables cats to remove the sheaths of their nails as the new nail grows in and to mark objects with their scent using glands on providing posts made of carpet, sisal rope, or wood is an effective way to save wear and tear on your furniture and is a safe, painless alternative to declawing.

Your Exotic Shorthair will spend up to 16 hours a day sleeping and may want to snuggle with you when you hit the sack. You might be flattered and encourage her to do so. Even if your cat has a welcome sleeping place in your bed, providing other sleeping areas around the house will help your cat feel at home and may keep cat hair from accumulating on your furniture. Cats love to sleep in tight, cozy

Scratching is a favorite feline occupation and keeps a cat's claws sharp. Ch. Arealand's Clarice, at eight weeks of age, owned by Gil Arellanes.

places. Fake fur kitty cups and molded beds enable your cat to curl up inside for a good night's sleep or a quick catnap. Soft foam beds that can be placed on a chair or sofa keep your cat's spirits up and cat hair deposits down. Beds can be as simple as a fabric-covered piece of foam or as elaborate as a double-decker

bunk bed. You will find them in colors to match any decor.

Food and water bowls come in glass, aluminum, plastic, ceramic, and china. Plastic has an advantage in that it won't break, but plastic accumulates oils that are more difficult to remove and may exacerbate a case of feline acne—black crusty patches on a cat's chin. If you purchase ceramic or china bowls, make certain that they are lead free. Because cats don't typically drink water with their meals, avoid combination bowls that have food and water sections joined together. Place your cat's water dish away from her food bowl in another part of the kitchen or in another room altogether to encourage drinking.

Playtime will be an important part of your interaction with your Exotic Shorthair. Provide her with safe toys to occupy her time, with or without you. Interactive toys enable her to get exercise and have fun. Toys need not be expensive, either. A cat will enjoy chasing a crumpled piece of paper or sliding in a paper

Your Exotic will spend up to 16 hours a day sleeping, so providing her with a tight, cozy place to snuggle into will make her feel right at home. Ch. Sweetpeacats Bit-O-Honey (female) and Sweetpeacats Apollo (male), four months old, owned by Grace Thomas.

sack with no handles as much as playing with a more costly, complex apparatus.

SAFETY

Keeping your cat indoors will prevent certain accidents from happening, but your home is not totally safe unless you take steps to make it so. Many houseplants are poisonous to cats. Ingesting them can cause symptoms that range from stomach upset and vomiting to coma and death. The list of poisonous plants is extensive, so ask your veterinarian for one and eliminate any from your home or place them out of your cat's reach. To provide your cat with a fresh supply of greens, plant some grass seed in a small container for her to chew.

Cats like to snuggle in warm places, so keep dryer and oven doors closed. Many cats have suffocated and died because their owners didn't know they were in the dryer when clothes were put in and the machine turned on.

Keep harmful chemicals and medicines out of your cat's reach. Mothballs, cleansers, cleaning products, and human prescription or nonprescription drugs can be fatal to the cat that swallows them. When cleaning, remove any residue of the cleaning product to prevent your Exotic Shorthair from getting any on her coat then licking it off. Cats are drawn to antifreeze, so clean up any that has spilled in your garage. Antifreeze with propylene glycol instead of ethylene glycol is safer, but is still toxic if enough is ingested.

Tie up loose electrical cords if your cat seems to want to chew on them. Don't allow miniblind cords or drapery pulls to dangle and entice your kitten or cat to play and accidentally get caught in them. Keep small objects, such as needles, pins, coins, and paperclips out of sight. One of the major causes of death, particularly for city cats, is falling from an open window. Even a fall from a second-story window may be fatal, so be sure to keep screens securely fastened or windows closed.

GROOMING

The Exotic Shorthair has been called the "lazy man's Persian," because caring for her shorter coat is less time-consuming than for that of her Persian cousin. However, your Exotic Shorthair will still have to be groomed regularly, and you can expect her to shed all year long. Because cats love to wash themselves, you may wonder why this grooming is necessary. The reason is that grooming will help keep loose hair to a minimum and help prevent your cat from getting hairballs. These nuisances are wads of swallowed hair that form clumps

Playtime is an important part of your interaction with your Exotic Shorthair. Provide her with safe toys to occupy her time when she's with or without you.

Many houseplants are poisonous to cats. Ask your veterinarian which ones you need to eliminate from your home or place out of your cat's reach.

that a cat expels by vomiting or that can become lodged in her digestive tract and cause blockage problems. Grooming will also help you detect any fleas and discover allergic reactions that may result in skin problems or bald patches.

Basic grooming tools include a soft-bristle brush, metal-toothed comb, cat toothbrush and toothpaste, cat shampoo, and nail clippers. Combining home health exams with weekly grooming sessions are a good way to keep on top of your cat's physical condition.

Exotic Shorthairs have a thick double coat of hair that gives them their plush look. Even though your grooming chores will be lighter than had you adopted a Persian, your Exotic Shorthair will

Keeping your cat indoors and catproofing your home will keep your Exotic safe and prevent many accidents from happening. Arealand's Wine Country Spirit, owned by Gil Arellanes.

shed all year long. Undercoat rakes that are typically used on cats with thick undercoats pull out and remove parts of the undercoat to prevent it from knotting. An undercoat on an Exotic Shorthair, however, is necessary for competing in the show ring, so don't use an undercoat rake if you plan to show your Exotic Shorthair.

four paws. Before bathing your cat, use a nail clipper specifically made for trimming cats' nails. Hold your cat's paw and spread her toes. Look at the nails. You will notice that each has a pink area closer to the nail base. This is called the "quick." When you trim the nails, it is extremely important not to trim down to the quick. Trimming there is

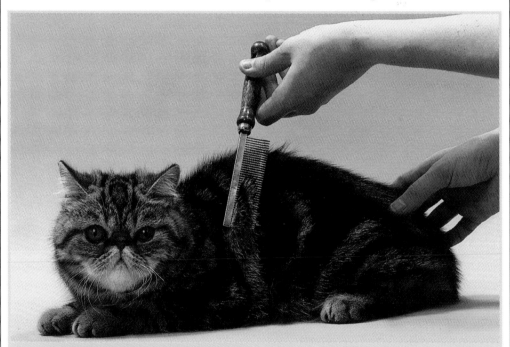

Regular weekly grooming will keep your Exotic's plush, double coat healthy and soft and is a good way to keep on top of your cat's physical condition.

Instead, use a long-toothed, steel comb to remove any clumped hair with a minimum of hair loss and to give your cat that light, fluffy look that is so desirable in the breed.

Your Exotic Shorthair kitten may keep her nails trimmed by scratching them on the post you've provided, but if you are entering a cat show, you will be required to clip her nails on all

extremely painful to a cat and can cause the nail to bleed.

Once your cat's nails are trimmed, move on to the bath. Cats often show an aversion to bathing, but if you are planning on exhibiting your Exotic Shorthair, you will need to bathe and groom her before each show. The sooner you begin getting her accustomed to the process, the better off both of you will be.

During the bath, relax and make the experience a positive one for your cat or kitten. When bathing your cat, use only a mild shampoo intended for use on cats and kittens. Make sure the room temperature is warm enough for your cat during her bath and afterward when you towel her dry. Have clean towels handy. Fill a sink or small dishpan with warm water. If you want, put a bath mat on the bottom so your cat won't slide. Allow your cat to get used to standing in the water. You might want to just go this far a few times before you actually wash her. When you are applying shampoo and working up a lather, keep it out of your cat's eyes and ears. Use a washcloth on her face and make sure you wash between your cat's toes and her hindquarters. The shorter noses of the Exotic Shorthair and her Persian cousin may result in a crimped tear duct, which requires daily facial cleaning in addition to her regular bath. Rinse thoroughly and repeat. Thoroughly dry your cat with a blow dryer or a drying cage.

If you like, use a cream rinse or conditioner on your cat after her bath. These will make her hair feel silky and help prevent dryness. Use only products intended for use on cats. Products intended for people and for dogs can be toxic to your cat.

A thorough teeth cleaning should be part of your cat's annual checkup, but you will need to help in between times. Your veterinarian will be able to supply you with a toothbrush and toothpaste intended for cats. Using it regularly and before a show will contribute to the cat's overall health and well-being.

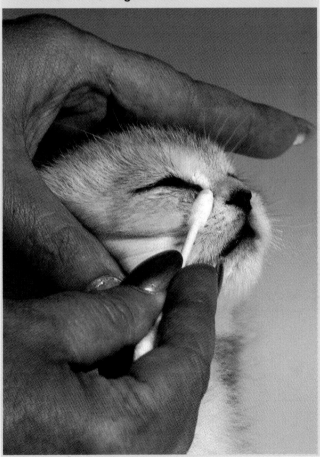

The shorter noses of the Exotic may result in a crimped tear duct, so daily facial cleaning is required in addition to her regular bath.

FEEDING

Up until the age of six to eight weeks, a cat's nutritional requirements are met by her mother. Once a kitten is weaned, it becomes the responsibility of her human caregiver to provide her with a nutritional diet to ensure growth into a healthy, happy adult cat and to maintain the cat's health through the remaining stages of her life. Cats have a reputation for being finicky eaters, and what may turn on the taste buds of one feline may, in fact, turn up the nose of another. Given all of the choices of commercial and premium cat food these days, it should be relatively easy for you to find a variety of foods to keep your Exotic Shorthair healthy and happy.

The standards by which pet food is tested and how pet food is labeled are regulated by the Association of American Feed Control Officials (AAFCO), who determine not only what goes on a label but the order in which it is presented. Reading the labels of cat food can be confusing, but it is the best way to determine whether it meets the stringent standards set up to provide your cat with optimum nutrition. Cat food that is complete and nutritionally balanced will have a

Up to six or eight weeks of age, a kitten's nutritional needs are met by her mother. Once weaned, her human caregiver is responsible for providing her with a healthy diet. Sweetpeacats Cindy and her two-month-old babies, owned by Grace Thomas.

guarantee on the label that reads, "Animal feeding tests using AAFCO procedures substantiate that *(brand name)* provides complete and balanced nutrition for all life stages of cats."

NUTRIENTS

Just like you, cats need certain nutrients to maintain their bodies' found in animal sources for optimum health. Cats are carnivores as a result of tens of thousands of years of evolution. Because of their unique metabolisms, they require from two to three times the digestible protein of their canine counterparts. Good-quality commercial food will indicate that

Unlike humans, who can exist on a vegetarian diet, a cat has a digestive system that requires animal-based protein for optimum health.

systems: protein, water, carbohydrates for energy, dietary fat, vitamins, and minerals. Unlike you, who could exist on a vegetarian diet that contains protein only from non-meat sources, the cat has a digestive system that requires protein it contains as primary ingredients protein from meat, poultry and its by-products, or from seafood.

Protein is the source of amino acids, which are a major component of body tissue. One of the essential amino acids, taurine, has received much attention in recent years because lack of it can result in feline heart and eye problems. Most commercial foods now have taurine added to the product.

Like all mammals, cats require *water* to facilitate all of their bodily processes. Cats fulfill some of their water requirements from the food they eat. More water is found in canned (or wet) cat food than that of dry, so a cat eating only dry food will most likely consume more water than one eating a diet of wet food, or one that combines the wet and dry varieties.

Because today's domestic cat evolved from an ancestor that lived in the desert of northern Africa, she is able to withstand dehydration better than you or your pet dog. Normal bodily functions, such as urination, defecation, and perspiration, cause your Exotic to lose water that must be replaced with fresh water daily. A freshly filled bowl somewhere other than next to your Exotic's food dish will be a well-liked watering hole. Some cats prefer their water cold, so you may find your Exotic soliciting you to turn on the bathroom faucet or imploring you to share the jug of spring water in the refrigerator rather than partaking of water that is room temperature.

Carbohydrates in the form of sugars and starches are a source of energy that help a cat

Cats don't typically drink water with their meals, so to encourage drinking, keep your Exotic's water dish away from her food bowl in the kitchen or in another room.

metabolize other nutrients and maintain body temperature, activity level, growth, and reproduction. Although your cat can obtain adequate amounts of energy from protein and fat, most commercial pet foods contain carbohydrates.

The *fat* contained in cat food provides your Exotic with energy and makes its food more palatable. Fat also supplies essential fatty acids, which enable

Proper nutrition for your cat is always important. Your feline friend can reap the benefits of ultimate nutrition with healthy skin, a shiny coat, bright eyes, playful energy, and all-around good health. Photo courtesy of Nutro Products, Inc.

your cat to metabolize the fat-soluble vitamins, A, D, E, and K. Dietary fat will help your cat maintain a healthy, shiny coat, heal wounds, and fight infection.

Your Exotic needs *vitamins* for metabolism of other nutrients and for growth and maintenance. Although too little vitamin content in a cat's diet can cause health problems, too much of certain vitamins can do the same. The body uses water-soluble vitamins, such as B complex, niacin, and thiamin, and eliminates excess

quantities. Amounts of vitamins, A, D, E, and K that are not used immediately in the digestive process are stored in the body's fat. Because too much A and D can cause toxicity, veterinarians do not recommend that you give your cat supplements unless you are advised to do so because of a health problem.

Your Exotic Shorthair requires *minerals* to aid in bone growth, tooth formation, blood clotting, basic metabolism, muscle function, anemia prevention, cell oxygenation, and proper functioning of the thyroid gland. Minerals work in combination with one another, and, like the other essential nutrients, are present in quantities meeting recommended allowances in good commercial and premium cat foods.

TYPES OF FOOD

In addition to a vast array of cat food brands, cats and their owners may choose among three types of food as well. Although they differ in the way they are processed by pet food manufacturers, all three types can provide adequate nutrition for your Exotic Shorthair, so read the labels carefully.

Wet—or canned—food is generally more expensive than the other types of cat food, but it is more palatable, especially if your cat is a finicky eater. Because it may contain more than 75 percent water, canned food is a good dietary source of this essential nutrient. Canned food is available in sizes from 2.5 ounces to 14 ounces. Although unopened cans have a lengthy shelf life, uneaten portions must be refrigerated to maintain freshness.

Semi-moist cat food is less costly than canned but has more preservatives added to prevent spoilage of the product once the container has been opened. Many cat owners find semi-moist cat food more convenient, because it can be kept for longer periods than canned food and can be free-fed to a cat without fear of it becoming contaminated as quickly as canned.

Treats can be provided on an occasional basis to help provide a little variety in the diet. Some treats act as a cleansing agent to help reduce tartar on a cat's teeth. Photo courtesy of Heinz.

Dry is the most economical type of cat food. Because of its minimal water content, cats eat less of it in volume than either the wet or semi-moist varieties. Dry food may be free-fed to a cat without the fear of it attracting insects or becoming rancid when exposed to the air. Chewing dry food also aids your Exotic in keeping her teeth clean.

Regardless of the type of food you decide to feed your cat, variety is important to prevent her from relying on a food that may not be nutritionally complete. Protein should come from a mixture of meat, poultry, or fish to avoid deficiencies that might develop from consuming food from only one source—such as organ meats, red meat, or fish, for example.

HOW MUCH TO FEED

The Exotic Shorthair has a muscular, cobby body, but her size and weight may vary from cat to cat. You will want to feed a quantity that is appropriate for your cat. Many factors can affect the quantity of food your Exotic requires on a daily basis, including her activity level, overall condition, age, type of food, and so forth. An active kitten or young cat will require a higher caloric intake than a less active adult or senior.

The bottom line is that your Exotic Shorthair's calorie intake should match her calorie expenditure. Counting calories for your cat can be as cumbersome and problematic as counting them for yourself, so using a basic rule of thumb will help guide you in determining correct quantities. Every cat has a layer of subcutaneous fat, but you should be able to feel the rib cage beneath the skin. A cat should not be so thin that her bones show nor so fat that you cannot feel her ribs. If you can't, your Exotic may be overweight and should be placed on a weight reduction program.

On cat food labels,

An active kitten or young cat will require a higher calorie intake than a less active adult or senior. One-month old Ch. Sweetpeacats Jim Dandy, owned by Grace Thomas.

manufacturers offer guidelines for how much of their product to feed a cat. If you are feeding more than one type of food to your Exotic, she will require less of each kind than the suggested quantity.

A more recent development in pet food products are those that have been developed for cats of different ages. You will be able to find a wide variety of foods for kittens, adult cats, and seniors. If your Exotic Shorthair develops a health problem as she ages, such as feline lower urinary tract disease (LUTD) or kidney disease, discuss the options with your veterinarian. He will be able to recommend a food product to help your cat combat her illness.

Before bringing home your Exotic kitten or cat, find out from the breeder or previous owner what she was fed. If you want to alter her diet, do so gradually to prevent stress or diet-related problems, such as diarrhea, due to a sudden change in food.

HEALTH CARE

One of your primary responsibilities as a cat owner will be to provide your Exotic Shorthair kitten or cat with good veterinary care. Preventing problems before they start is always the best medicine, and annual veterinary checkups, along with good nutrition, will parasites or blood tests to detect contagious diseases. Your veterinarian will find most potential problems early enough to treat them. You can aid in the effort throughout the year by performing home health exams. Closely observe your Exotic Shorthair's condition and

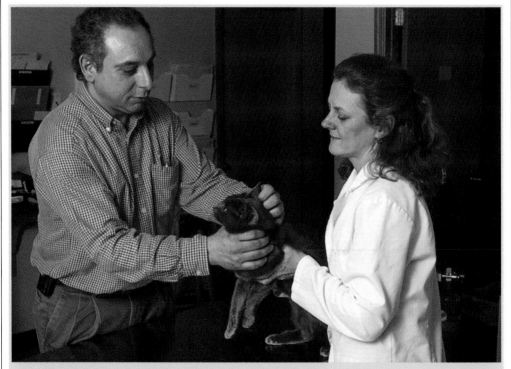

Annual veterinary checkups, along with good nutrition, will help keep your Exotic Shorthair fit and healthy.

help you keep your Exotic Shorthair fit and healthy. A complete physical exam includes weighing your cat; examining her eyes, ears, and mouth, teeth, and gums; feeling for fluid buildup or bumps under the skin; and performing some simple tests, such as a fecal examination to detect internal behavior to detect problems early and, if necessary, seek medical attention.

RECOGNIZING AN ILL CAT

Cats are adept at concealing illness and hiding any discomfort they may feel to anyone but the most astute observer, so learning the danger signs of disease will greatly help you to protect your cat. Being able to describe a symptom will help your veterinarian diagnose the problem. Different illnesses may have similar symptoms, so the more detail you can provide your veterinarian, the better the chance for a positive outcome. Illness may reveal itself in both subtle or not-so-subtle behavioral changes, which may preclude overt physical signs that a health problem exists.

Cats occasionally turn their noses up at the food their owners offer them, but if your cat seems disinterested in her meals altogether, it could signal a

Aside from physical signs, behavioral changes like excessive sleeping, hiding, or loss of interest in playthings can signal that a health problem exists.

problem. If she does not eat for more than a day or exhibits other symptoms as well, contact your veterinarian. If your Exotic Shorthair is drinking more than usual or sitting with her head hanging over the water dish, it could be a sign of dehydration due to a fever, ingestion of a toxin, or kidney problems, among other possibilities.

Changes in litter box habits, such as urinating or defecating out of the box, are often thought to be behavior problems, but they may signal that something is physically wrong, such as lower urinary tract disease or intestinal blockage. If your Exotic Shorthair suddenly exhibits an aversion to the litter box, have the cat examined by your veterinarian first before trying a behavior modification program.

If your quiet, gentle Exotic Shorthair turns suddenly aggressive or antisocial for no apparent reason, something physical may be the problem. Other behavioral changes that may mean your cat doesn't feel well include sleeping more than usual, hiding, crying for no apparent reason, listlessness, and loss of interest in playthings and people.

Physical signs of illness may include vomiting or diarrhea. Cats often will vomit up a hairball or food if it does not agree with them. Likewise, they may occasionally have loose bowels. However, if the vomiting is repeated, or the diarrhea lasts for more than a day, or if you notice blood in your Exotic Shorthair's stools or urine, see your veterinarian. Cats that are ill lose their desire to wash, and a dull, lifeless coat is one of the first signs that something may be wrong. If your cat is continually licking herself or washing so much that bald patches appear on her skin, it could indicate external parasites or allergies. Other overt physical signs of illness include wheezing, gagging, retching, sneezing, tearing or watery discharge from the eyes or nose, limping, hair loss or weight loss, seizures or fits, and lumps or bumps on or under the skin.

VACCINATIONS

As part of her annual checkup, your veterinarian will vaccinate your Exotic Shorthair against the more common feline diseases. Vaccines will force your cat's immune system to generate specialized proteins, called antibodies, that will help her develop resistance to bacteria, viruses, or toxins and fight off disease. By being exposed to the particular disease antigens, your Exotic Shorthair's immune system will fight off offending contagions if she should come into contact with them. Because your cat's immunity can decrease over time, she must be revaccinated, usually annually, at the time of her veterinary checkup.

If your Exotic Shorthair kitten has not been vaccinated already by the breeder from whom you obtained it, your veterinarian will administer a three-way series of shots called FVRCP. The shots typically are given in a series of two to three shots at three-week intervals starting at the age of six to eight weeks.

Respiratory Diseases

FVRCP vaccines help your cat fight off feline viral rhinotracheitis (FVR) and feline calicivirus (FCV), two of the more common and contagious respiratory diseases that infect cats. Both FVR and FCV account for the majority of feline respiratory diseases. Symptoms may include sneezing,

As part of her annual checkup, your veterinarian will vaccinate your Exotic against common feline diseases.

coughing, and discharge from the nose and eyes. A cat with upper respiratory disease can become dehydrated and lose her appetite. Respiratory viruses live outside the body of an animal for several hours to several days and can be transmitted from one cat to another through direct contact with an infected cat, contaminated cages, food and water dishes, bedding, and even the litter box of an ailing cat.

Feline Distemper

The third component of the vaccine will help your cat's immune system fight feline panleukopenia (FP) or, as it's more commonly called, feline distemper, a highly contagious viral disease characterized by fever, loss of appetite, dehydration, vomiting, and a decrease in white blood cells. Like the previous viruses, feline panleukopenia virus can be transmitted through direct contact with an infected cat, through contact with contaminated objects such as food bowls, litter pans, or bedding, and by fleas. Kittens, because of their underdeveloped immune systems, are at greatest risk of contracting feline panleukopenia.

Rabies

Rabies is caused by a virus that attacks the central nervous system of warm-blooded animals, and it can be transmitted from one species of animal to another.

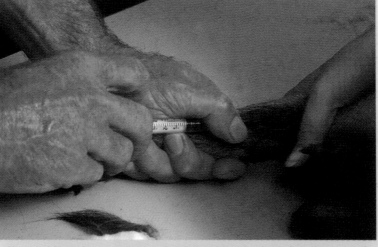

If your kitten has not been vaccinated by the breeder, the vet will administer a series of shots called FVRCP at three-week intervals, beginning at the age of six to eight weeks.

Your Exotic Shorthair cat can get rabies from the bite of a rabid animal or through infected saliva entering the body through an open wound, the eyes, or the mouth. The end result of rabies infection is death. Keeping your Exotic Shorthair indoors will help prevent her from contracting rabies and other contagious diseases. Vaccinations will provide an extra measure of protection. Depending on where you live, you may be required by law to have your cat vaccinated against rabies and to obtain booster shots every one to three years.

Other Contagious Diseases

If you obtained your Exotic Shorthair kitten or cat from a reputable breeder, it should be free of contagious diseases at the time of purchase. Reputable breeders routinely test their cats for contagious diseases to prevent them from accidentally spreading disease to other cats in their catteries and also to prevent breeding stock from afflicting their offspring.

Feline Leukemia Virus

Feline leukemia virus (FLV) impairs a cat's immune system, makes her more susceptible to contracting other illnesses, and decreases her ability to fight off the effects of the disease. FLV is transmitted primarily via saliva and respiratory secretions, urine, and feces. Social grooming and licking and sharing litter boxes, food, and water bowls easily transmit the leukemia virus from one cat to another in a multicat household. Cats roaming outdoors risk exposure via bite wounds from infected cats. A queen can transmit feline leukemia virus to her offspring during pregnancy or while nursing the kittens. Symptoms of FLV are often nonspecific. Poor coat appearance, loss of appetite and subsequent weight loss, lethargy, and stunted growth are some of the more common ones.

Pet owners should be aware that social grooming and the sharing of food bowls, litter boxes, and bedding can easily transmit diseases and parasites from one cat to another in a multicat household. Ch. Arealand's Clarice, owned by Gil Arellanes.

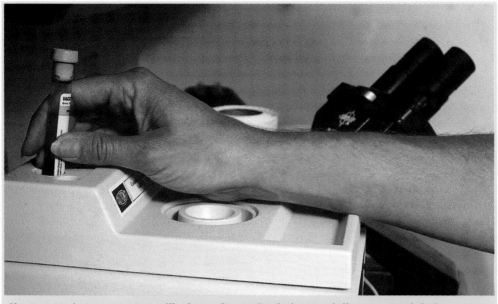

If your cat shows symptoms like loss of appetite, lethargy, dull coat, or weight loss, tests are available that can determine whether or not your pet has contracted a disease or virus.

Nearly one-third of cats exposed to feline leukemia virus develop a natural immunity to the disease and never become ill. Others may become latent carriers—either never succumbing to the effects of the disease or showing symptoms only under conditions such as stress or the onset of other diseases. The remaining FLV-positive cats die from the effects of the virus, usually within three years. A test is available to detect FLV. If your Exotic Shorthair tests positive, have her retested within three to four weeks. If the resulting tests are negative, discuss vaccination options against feline leukemia virus with your veterinarian.

Feline Infectious Peritonitis

Feline infectious peritonitis (FIP) is a contagious and deadly disease that, like feline leukemia, has no cure. Laboratory tests can detect the presence of antibodies to coronaviruses—of which FIP is one—but cannot specifically identify the FIP virus. Cats with the "wet" type of FIP will look extremely bloated in the abdominal area. If fluid buildup occurs in the chest cavity, respiratory problems may occur. Other signs of FIP may include fever, loss of appetite, weight loss, and depression. Even in catteries and multicat households, FIP is fairly uncommon. Most cats that contract FIP also have other immune-suppressing conditions such as feline leukemia. There is a vaccine available to prevent FIP, but it has aroused much controversy since its introduction. If you keep your cat indoors and away from other cats with an unknown health status, you greatly lessen her chances of contracting FIP.

Feline Immunodeficiency Virus

Feline immunodeficiency virus (FIV), commonly referred to as "feline AIDS," is another immune-suppressing virus for which there is no cure. Although the virus is similar to immune-suppressing viruses in other species, including HIV, which affects humans, it cannot be passed from cat to person or vice versa.

Transmission of FIV is thought presence of the feline immunodeficiency virus, but there is no vaccine available to prevent the disease. Keeping your cat indoors and away from infected cats is the best preventive measure you can take.

PARASITES

Parasites are organisms that obtain their food by living on or in a host animal, very often at the

Keeping your Exotic away from cats of unknown health status is the best preventive measure you can take to keep her healthy. Ch. Jamkatsmeow Thunder and Ch. Jamkatsmeow Silver of Sweetpeacats, owned by Grace Thomas.

to be through bite wounds from infected cats. Symptoms of FIV are difficult to pinpoint, because a host of secondary infections, such as anemia and low white blood cell count, can occur. Mouth and teeth problems, such as gingivitis, stomatitis, and periodontis, are often the first signs of feline immunodeficiency virus. An antibody test will confirm the expense of the host's health and well-being. The more common external parasites to afflict cats include fleas, mites, and ticks.

Fleas

Among these parasites, the most common and frustrating are fleas. If they make a home with you and your Exotic Shorthair, you may find them the most difficult to expel, because not only must you eliminate the adult fleas, but also the eggs and larvae, which can live up to two years in your furniture and carpet. If your Exotic Shorthair has become infested with fleas, you will notice flea dirt—bits of flea feces, ingested blood, and eggs—accumulating wherever your cat may sit or sleep. Fleas lay more eggs during warmer, more humid months, making them especially devastating

If your Exotic excessively shakes her head, scratches her ears, or becomes restless, she may have ear mites, which can be treated easily with medication.

Keeping your cat indoors will reduce the risk of her contracting fleas or other parasites, although it is no guarantee. Be sure to check your Exotic's coat on a regular basis.

during the summer or in warmer climates. Fleas not only are painful and annoying to cats, they can also produce an allergic reaction, resulting in excessive licking and biting and subsequent hair loss. Keeping your Exotic Shorthair indoors will reduce the risk of her contracting fleas, but it is no guarantee. Even an indoor cat can get fleas, which may be carried in from the yard on your clothing or on other pets.

To prevent fleas, new products in pill or liquid form have come on the market in recent years that, when given regularly, damage the flea eggs and disrupt their life cycle. A wide variety of flea products, such as sprays, powders, dips, shampoos, soaps, and disposable dampened topical cloths, are available to rid your Exotic Shorthair of fleas. Be sure to follow package directions, and never mix products or use flea products intended for dogs on your cat. To eliminate fleas from the environment, foggers, misters, or premises sprays will help remove them from floors, bedding, carpet, and furniture.

Ear Mites

Ear mites, which appear as a brown, caked substance in a cat's ears, are microscopic parasites that can make your Exotic

Shorthair shake her head, scratch her ears, or become restless. Although ear mites are annoying to your cat, they can be treated relatively easily and eliminated with medication.

Tapeworm and Other Internal Parasites

If your cat eats infected fleas while grooming herself or decides to have an infected mouse, frog, or snake for her dinner, chances are she will develop one of three kinds of tapeworm—an internal parasite that can grow up to two feet in length in your cat's body. You most likely

The only reason to ever let your cat remain unaltered is if she is part of a legitimate breeding program associated with pedigreed cat registries, or if you plan to show your animal in competition. Ch. Caliope's Wayfarer, owned by Grace Thomas.

won't notice a tapeworm until tiny segments of worm resembling rice or sesame seeds are expelled. Your veterinarian will be able to treat the tapeworm, but you must rid your cat and your house of the fleas or other root causes to prevent them from recurring. Tapeworms, like all parasites, can rob your cat of her nutrition or result in a weakened immune system if they are not eliminated from your cat's body.

Other internal parasites include roundworms, hookworms, and heartworms. To detect internal parasites, your veterinarian will conduct a fecal exam as part of your cat's annual checkup. He or she will prescribe appropriate medicine to get rid of them.

SPAYING AND NEUTERING

One of the kindest things you can do for your Exotic Shorthair and yourself is to have her spayed, if a female, or neutered, if a male. The only reason ever to let your cat remain unaltered is if she is part of a legitimate breeding program associated with one of the pedigreed cat registries. To breed your cat simply to generate income, allow a female to experience producing a litter, or allow your children to experience the miracle of birth does a disservice to you, your cat, and cats everywhere. No matter how careful a breeder you are, you cannot prevent the possibility of adding to the already overwhelming homeless cat problem. Breeding purebred cats is best left to full-time breeders.

Neutering

Neutering a tom is a relatively simple procedure. Although

Spaying is a common and safe procedure during which the uterus of the female is removed.

performed under anesthetic, neutering is usually done on an outpatient basis, and the cat is allowed to return home the same day as the surgery. Leaving your male intact will promote a host of behaviors that are unpleasant for the owner as well as anyone visiting the home. Unneutered males mark territory by spraying an anal gland secretion that produces an offensive odor that is difficult to remove or mask. Once the odor is in your home, it will perpetuate itself by arousing your male to continue to mark things around the house, not only when he detects the presence of an unspayed female, but also when he detects the presence of any other cat from which he wants to protect his territory. Once a male begins to spray, this habit is more difficult

to break, but neutering will help prevent this behavior from ever occurring.

Spaying

Spaying is a procedure during which the uterus of the female is removed. Although it is more complex than neutering, spaying is a common procedure and is no cause for concern. The female usually remains in the veterinary hospital for one to three days following surgery and returns about ten days later for removal of stitches. As with male cats, unaltered females engage in behavior that most owners have difficulty enduring. When an intact female enters estrus—

Veterinarians are altering cats at earlier ages, but the procedure should be performed no later than six to eight months of age.

the period of time when she is receptive to a male for the purposes of reproduction—she will engage in behavior that is sexually suggestive to the male cat but very annoying to her human companions. Rolling, crying, walking around with her posterior in the air, urinating more often, and dribbling watery

FELINE FIRST AID

Keeping your cat indoors and catproofing your home will prevent a lot of accidents from ever happening, but sometimes even your best efforts won't make any difference. Cats don't always land on their feet, so falling or slipping can be a problem even inside the home.

If your Exotic sustains an injury from an accident or fall, acting quickly and appropriately may help save your cat's life.

discharge throughout her environment are some of the behaviors owners of unspayed females must suffer. Veterinarians are altering cats at earlier ages, but the procedure should be performed no later than six to eight months of age. Discuss with your veterinarian the appropriate time to neuter or spay your cat.

Ingesting a household chemical, falling out of an upper-story window, chewing on an electrical wire, getting caught in a miniblind cord, burning paws on a hot surface, or even getting too close to a candle flame are all examples of potential accidents. Being prepared might help save your cat's life in case one of these unfortunate events occurs.

If your Exotic Shorthair sustains an accident, a knowledge of first aid will help you deal with the situation. Keep your cool. Don't wait until an emergency happens to hunt for appropriate phone numbers or determine how you should deal with the situation. Acting quickly and appropriately may help save your cat's life. Keep your veterinarian's phone number and the number of an off-hours emergency clinic near your telephone with other emergency numbers in case you need them. Purchase a book on feline first aid techniques and put together a first aid kit. Keep both handy.

Preventing problems before they start is always the best medicine. Perform regular home exams to detect problems early.

EXOTIC SHORTHAIR HEALTH ISSUES

Reputable breeders attest to the Exotic Shorthair being a hardy breed. Queens usually have three to four in a litter, and very few are ever lost due to health problems. Because the Exotic Shorthair's face is shortened like her Persian cousin, her jaw may develop at a different rate than is usual, causing the teeth to grow out of alignment. Irregularities associated with an asymmetrical jaw can lead to dental problems, including the necessity of having an occasional tooth removed by a veterinarian. This can cause an otherwise excellent show prospect to be relegated to pet status.

EXHIBITING EXOTIC SHORTHAIRS

As the owner of an Exotic Shorthair, you will sooner or later find yourself drawn to the world of the cat fancy, whether as an active participant (exhibiting your cat in shows) or as a spectator. Even if your Exotic Shorthair is a pet-quality cat rather than a show-quality one, you are eligible to exhibit her in a cat show and compete with other pet-quality cats. Cat shows are events at which breeders, cat owners, and cat product vendors can literally show off their wares. For the spectator, cat shows provide ample opportunities to learn about cats, new cat-related products, and what constitutes a superb specimen of the breed.

ASSOCIATIONS AND CLUBS

There are several pedigreed cat associations in the US plus Canada and many more worldwide that promote the cat fancy through regularly held shows. Even registries based in the US can boast international members and shows held on foreign soil. Recordkeeping is a primary function of the registries that maintain the pedigrees of the cats and kittens of its members and guarantee that future offspring can be registered and ancestors traced. Some registries allow individual memberships, while others offer membership through regional or local cat clubs affiliated with the national association.

Exotic Shorthair breeders have a national organization that is

Cat shows provide opportunities to learn about cats and what constitutes a superior example of the breed. Ch. Sweetpeacats Classic, owned by Grace Thomas.

affiliated with the Cat Fanciers' Association. The regional clubs as well as the registries are nonprofit organizations whose goals center around promoting the cat fancy, the improvement of the individual breeds they recognize, and the welfare of cats in general. The Cat Fanciers' Association, for example, supports the Robert H. Winn

volunteers at local animal shelters. Registries have breed councils or committees that serve as advisory bodies to the national associations. The Exotic Shorthair breed organizations are comprised of people knowledgeable about and experienced in the breed and are responsible for the continued development of the breed and for

Producing cats that are superb specimens of the standard for the breed is something breeders aspire to, and shows provide an ideal place to exhibit them. Bill Thomas and Elita McNeil of Incats.

Foundation, a nonprofit corporation that awards grants to research feline health-related studies and sponsors an annual symposium on current feline veterinary topics. Pedigreed cat registries take an active part in the community to encourage spay/neuter awareness, and their members become active

obtaining approval for modifications to the breed standard.

SHOWS

Cat shows are the heart of the cat fancy. Producing cats that conform to the standards of the breed is something to which all breeders aspire, and the cat show provides the opportunity for them to exhibit not only the fruits of their labor but also to compete with their peers for awards and prizes. The first cat show, which resulted in the birth of the cat fancy, took place in London's Crystal Palace in 1871. It wasn't until 1895 that a show held in New York City's Madison Square Garden brought the cat fancy to the US. Cat shows may be one-, two- or several-day events, depending on the size of the sponsoring club, and they are classified as all-breed shows in which all breeds and types of cats compete for awards, or specialty shows in which only cats of a particular type or coat length compete. Cat shows are held worldwide and are governed by the rules and regulations of the sanctioning registry. Even US-based associations sanction shows in foreign countries as well as international shows within the US. Attending an international show is quite an event. It can attract as many as 1,000 exhibitors from all over the world and as many as 10,000 visitors a day.

Judging

At a show, cats are judged in separate, independently running judging rings. Cats compete against the breed standard rather than against one another. Each judging ring is presided over by a judge who is trained and licensed by the association in either specific breeds and categories or all breeds and categories. Depending on the registry, categories may bear these names:

Championship: Unaltered, pedigreed cats eight months of age or older.

Premiership: Spayed or neutered cats eight months of age or older.

Kitten: Pedigreed kittens aged four to eight months.

Provisional or NBC (New Breed or Color): For breeds that have not yet achieved championship status.

AOV (Any Other Variety): Registered cats that do not conform to breed standards.

Household Pet: Mixed breed or non-pedigreed cats.

To the untrained eye, competition can seem complex and confusing. By the time a cat is entered in a show, it will already have been determined that the cat conforms to a great degree to the acceptable standard of the breed, and it will be the judge's job to determine which among many beautiful specimens comes closest. Before entering a show, it is wise to visit several as a spectator and watch the judging. Talk to exhibitors and familiarize yourself with the breed standard and categories in which you want to enter your Exotic Shorthair.

Registering

It is common practice in the cat registries to allow an unregistered kitten to compete in a show. Adult cats, to be eligible to compete, must be registered. Under The International Cat

Association (TICA) rules, an unregistered adult can enter a show one time before she must be registered with the association. The breeder from whom you purchased your kitten will have registered the litter when they were born. The registry will return certificates for the individual kittens to the breeder to be passed along to the buyer. The buyer returns the certificate and the appropriate fees with the cat's chosen name to the registry to complete the process. If you have purchased an adult cat from a breeder, he or she should give you the registration at the time of purchase.

Awards and Prizes

Each registry awards predefined types of ribbons for the various categories of awards. Once a cat has collected six first-place ribbons, she becomes a Champion, after which she is eligible to compete against other Champions to garner points for Grand and Supreme Grand Champion status. Prizes awarded include ribbons, trophies, and/or cash. Cats can register and compete in more than one registry, but points and

At a show, cats are judged against the breed standard rather than against one another. Ch. Arealand's Clarice, CFA show, 1997, owned by Gil Arellanes.

awards do not carry over from one registry to another. A competing cat has to start at square one and compete under the rules of the individual registry.

Entering a Show

Cat shows are held virtually year-round, and the dates, locations, and entry fees are advertised in the major cat publications, as well as on the web sites of the cat registries. Before entering, obtain a copy of the show rules, which describe entry procedures, eligibility, and exhibitor responsibility. After you have studied them, contact the entry clerk to request a show flyer and entry form. Send the completed form and fees by the deadline specified. You will receive confirmation by mail.

As you progress from local to national and international shows, the competition becomes steeper. The exhibition Exotic Shorthair must be an exemplary example of her breed and her coat in beautiful condition. She must be alert and playful, yet calm as she is being handled by the judge. Competing cats must be healthy, and in some cases, are required to have a veterinary inspection prior to the show. Your Exotic Shorthair must be free of contagious diseases. She must be well-behaved and able to withstand the stress and rigors of the show hall environment, which includes being caged for most of the day, being handled by judges whom she does not know, and tolerating the constant peering

eyes of show spectators.

Prior to the show, cats must be bathed and groomed and their nails clipped. Although the ears on most of today's Exotics are properly small, they appear to be larger than the Persian's, so before showing your Exotic, the hair on the tips of her ears and around her eyes may need to be clipped to conform to the Persian standard (except, of course, for the short coat).

At the Show Hall

Once at the show, your Exotic Shorthair will be assigned a number and a cage in what is called the benching area where cats await their turn in the judging ring. Shows typically involve a lot of commotion, but as an exhibitor you must pay attention to what is being announced over the public address system so that you don't miss being called. Cages are typically decorated and carry the cattery name if the cats inside are being shown by a breeder. They also may display ribbons already won by their occupants. In addition to any decorations you may want, you will need a carrier for your cat, a litter box, cat beds or blankets, food and water dishes, a supply of your cat's food and water, grooming tools, a first aid kit, paper towels, vaccination certificates, and show catalog. The show committee will provide cat litter.

If you decide to enter your cat in a show, or simply attend as a spectator, make the experience an enjoyable one.

A competing cat must be healthy, well-groomed, alert, and calm as she is handled by the judges and peered at by spectators.

HOW TO CONTACT THE REGISTRIES

The following are the major pedigreed cat registries in the US and Canada:

American Association of Cat Enthusiasts, Inc. (AACE)
Box 213
Pine Brook, IL 07058
913-335-6717
info@aaceinc.org
http://www.aaceinc.org

American Cat Association (ACA)
81901 Katherine Avenue
Panorama City, CA 91402
818-781-5656

American Cat Fanciers Association (ACFA)
P.O. Box 203
Point Lookout, MO 65726
417-334-5430
info@acfacat.com
http://www.acfacat.com/

Canadian Cat Association/(CCA) Association Feline Canadienne
220 Advance Blvd., Suite 101
Brampton, Ontario, Canada L6T 4J5
905-459-1481
office@cca-afc.com
http://www.cca-afc.com

Cat Fanciers' Association (CFA)
Box 1005
Manasquan, NJ 08736
cfa@cfainc.org
http://www.cfainc.org/

Cat Fanciers' Federation (CFF)
Box 661
Gratis, OH 45330
513-787-9009
http://www.cffinc.org/

The International Cat Association, Inc. (TICA)
Box 2684
Harlingen, TX 78551
210-428-8046
http://www.tica.org/

INDEX

INDEX